Funky Felt Crafts

★ American Girl®

Published by American Girl Publishing, Inc.

Questions or comments? Call 1-800-845-0005,
visit our Web site at **americangirl.com**,
or write to Customer Service, American Girl, 8400 Fairway Place, Middleton, WI 53562-0497.

Printed in China
09 10 11 12 13 14 15 LEO 10 9 8 7 6 5 4 3 2 1

All American Girl marks are trademarks of American Girl, LLC.

Editorial Development: Carrie Anton

Art Direction and Design: Camela Decaire

Production: Jeannette Bailey, Judith Lary, Sarah Boecher

Photography: Radlund Studios

Stylists: Carrie Anton, Camela Decaire, Jessica Hastreiter

Dear Reader,

What comes in bright colors, has no-fray edges, and can be used to create a ton of fun crafts? Felt! Inside this book, you'll find lots of ways to turn felt into great gifts, cuddly characters, faux food, and more! Filled with craft ideas and easy instructions, *Funky Felt Crafts* will give you the inspriration you need to make anything you can imagine using this unique fabric.

Your friends at American Girl

Felt Firsts

Use these tips to get started.

First Things First

Read through the directions carefully. If a project seems too difficult or when you see this hand , always ask an adult to help you.

Supplies

The supplies you'll need are listed with each craft. Be sure to gather all of your supplies before you begin. When working with messy supplies such as paint and glue, be sure to cover your workspace with newspaper. Here is a list of the basic items you'll need to do most of the crafts in this book:

- Felt
- Scissors
- Craft glue
- Glue stick
- Double-stick tape
- Embroidery needle
- Thread or embroidery floss

Patterns

The back of the book is filled with patterns you can use to make any of the crafts in this book. Each pattern is numbered, and that number is referenced in the craft's instructions. To use the patterns, trace them onto tracing paper or ask a parent to photocopy them. Cut the shape out and use it as a template on the felt. You can either trace the shape onto the felt, or use double-stick tape to hold the paper pattern to the felt so that you can cut around it.

Simple Knots

Starting Knot

1. Cut a length of thread. Wrap one end of the thread loosely around your finger three times.

2. Slip the thread off your finger and pass the other end of the thread through the open loop twice.

3. Pull the ends of the thread apart. This will create a knot. Trim the tail (if too long) and thread the needle.

Ending Knot

1. On your final stitch, repeat the stitch two or three times. In a hidden spot, pass the needle under this thicker stitch, creating a loop in the thread.

2. Pass the needle through the loop twice.

3. Pull tight. Trim excess thread.

 Because sewing needles are sharp, ask a parent to show you how to use them safely and help you when you do sewing crafts.

Simple Stitches

Starting Stitch

Begin whip and running stitches with a starting knot and threaded needle. At one edge of your project, pass the needle from the back of the material to the front. This hides your knot.

Whip Stitch

1. After your starting stitch, pass the needle again from the back of the material to the front, so that the thread shows over the edge.

2. Repeat step 1 until you have finished sewing the project area. Complete the stitches with an ending knot. Trim any excess thread.

Running Stitch

1. After your starting stitch, send the needle from front to back about ¼ or ½ inch from the needle's first spot.

2. Repeat step 1 on the back of the project, passing the needle from back to front. Space your stitches evenly.

3. Repeat steps 1 and 2 until you have finished sewing the project area. Complete the stitches with an ending knot.

Blanket Stitch

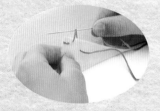

1. On the back of the project, send the needle through a small piece of the fabric to secure the knot.

2. With the thread wrapping from the back of the fabric to the front, insert the needle from front to back and pull through.

3. Pass the needle back through this loop from back to front and pull through.

4. Begin the next stitch about ½ inch from the previous stitch using the instructions in step 2.

5. Repeat steps 2 through 4 until you have finished sewing the project area. Complete the stitches with an ending knot.

Gifts

Cute Cards

Create heart-felt greetings.

You will need:
- Scrapbook paper
- Scissors
- Felt
- Glue or double-stick tape
- Embellishments (optional)

Cards can be made in all different shapes and sizes. Decorate the fronts of your cards using decorative shapes, letters, or animals cut from felt. Attach the felt using a small dab of glue or double-stick tape. If you like, attach additional embellishments, such as ribbon, buttons, or jewels.

Pretty Presents

Use felt to wrap gifts up right.

You will need:
- Box template
- Felt
- Glue stick or double-stick tape
- Scissors
- Embellishments (optional)

Punch out Box Template 1 or 2 from the back of the book. (You may want to create a copy of this before making this craft.) Attach the template to the felt using a glue stick or double-stick tape. Cut the felt around the shape, and fold the box using the perforated edges as guides. Decorate the box with additional felt cutouts or embellishments, such as ribbon or beads.

Beautiful Blooms

Pick the perfect petals to make a beautiful bouquet.

Folded

Cut a 2-by-4-inch rectangle from felt. Accordion-fold the felt lengthwise. Twist a chenille stem around the middle. Glue or staple the top and bottom ends of the felt on both sides to make a flower. Glue small black pom-poms to the middle, hiding the stem.

Rolled

Cut a 5-by-11-inch rectangle from felt. Place double-stick tape down one long end and fold the strip in half lengthwise. Cut 2-inch slits along the entire strip. Run a bead of glue along the strip and tightly roll. When glue is dry, knot a thin yellow felt strip and twist it around a chenille stem. String the chenille stem through the center of the flower.

Layered

Trace and cut out 3 Gerbera daisy shapes using Pattern 5.  With help from an adult, poke a brad through the center of each flower, layering the 3 shapes. Glue a chenille stem to the back of the flower, and fold down the ends of the brad so that the stem is secure.

Sewn

Trace and cut out Pattern 4. With a needle knotted and threaded, sew the ends of each petal to the middle. When all petals have been sewn, sew a button to the middle and end with a knot. Glue a chenille stem to the back of the flower.

Bubble Bag

Make this quick-sew bag with one simple stitch.

You will need:
- Felt
- Scissors
- Embroidery needle
- Embroidery floss
- 4 buttons
- 2 18-inch pieces of ribbon
- Patterns
- Glue
- Dimensional fabric paint

1. Cut out 2 9-by-9-inch shapes from felt; one will be the front of the bag and the other will be the back. Lay one piece on top of the other.

2. Using the Blanket Stitch (instructions on page 7), sew the edges of the bag together, starting at one top corner and working around to the other top corner. Leave one side open.

3. Attach each end of the handles by sandwiching the ribbon in between the button and one side of the bag and sewing the button and ribbon to the felt.

4. Trace and cut out circle shapes using Patterns 8–18 and 26. Glue the circles to the front of the bag. When glue is dry, use dimensional fabric paint to decorate the edges of each circle.

15

Sassy Scrapbook

Gather paper bags and friend photos to make a super scrapbook.

You will need:

- 4 small decorative paper bags (available at craft and party stores)
- Double-stick tape
- Ribbon
- Tape
- Scissors
- Felt
- Craft glue
- Appliqué (optional)
- Embellishments (optional)

1. Fold 1 paper bag in half with bottom of bag facing up. Repeat with other bags. Place double-stick tape along all 4 edges on top side of 1 folded bag.

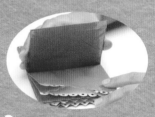

2. Attach the taped side to the folded top of another bag. Make sure that folded edges are on the same side and that all edges line up. Press to secure. Repeat with other bags.

3. Wrap ribbon around the pages and secure with tape. This will be the book closure. Make sure open ends of pages are not covered.

4. Cut felt to wrap around book to make cover. Glue felt to book. Let dry. Decorate cover and pages.

Blooming Belt

Turn pinches of felt into a garland of flowers.

You will need:
- Scissors
- Felt
- Thread
- Embroidery needle
- 2 pieces of ribbon
- Bead (optional)

1. To make 1 flower, cut a 1-by-5-inch rectangle from felt. Cut a long piece of thread and fold it in half. Thread both ends through the eye of the needle, leaving a loop at the other end.

2. Using the Running Stitch (instructions from page 6) without the starting knot, sew across the long side of the rectangle, leaving the loop as a tail.

3. When you reach the end of the strip, pass the needle through the hanging loop at the beginning of the strip and pull tightly so that the strip pinches together. Sew the edges together.

4. Repeat Steps 1–3 to make more flowers. Attach the flowers by sewing them together. Then sew the ribbons to each end. Decorate with a bead, if you like.

Cool Cuff Bracelet

Wrap your wrist in style!

You will need:
- Scissors
- Felt
- Ribbon
- Craft glue
- Patterns
- Embellishments (optional)
- Decorative-edge scissors (optional)

Cut out a rectangle of felt (at whatever width you like) long enough to fit around your wrist. Attach the ribbon to the cuff using craft glue. Or cut two small slits in the felt at each end to lace the ribbon ends through. Use the flower and circle patterns listed below to decorate your cuff. Glue on the shapes and any other embellishments.

Patterns 6, 7, 13, 14

Patterns 3, 13, 14

Creative Hair Clips

Turn whimsical shapes into great barrettes.

You will need:
- Pencil
- Scissors
- Felt
- Patterns
- Craft glue
- Ribbon
- Hair clips
- Dimensional fabric paint (optional)
- Embellishments (optional)

Trace and cut out fun shapes from felt using any of the patterns listed below. Using craft glue, attach a length of ribbon over each hair clip. To avoid fraying, fold the ends of the ribbon under before attaching to the hair clip. Decorate the hair clips by attaching the cutout shapes. Give the shapes pizzazz using dimensional fabric paint or embellishments such as buttons or beads.

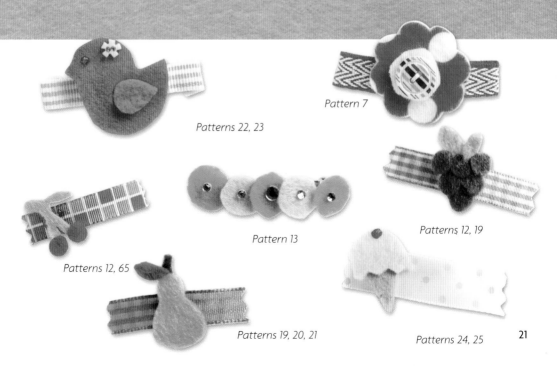

Patterns 22, 23

Pattern 7

Patterns 12, 65

Pattern 13

Patterns 12, 19

Patterns 19, 20, 21

Patterns 24, 25

21

Awesome Appliqués

Decorate your gear with fun felt critters!

You will need:
- Pencil
- Scissors
- Patterns
- Felt
- Craft glue or needle and thread
- Dimensional fabric paint (optional)
- Embellishments (optional)

Trace and cut out fun shapes from felt using various patterns listed below. Assemble the pieces using craft glue or by sewing. For more character, embellish the shapes with dimensional fabric paint, beads, buttons, or ribbon.

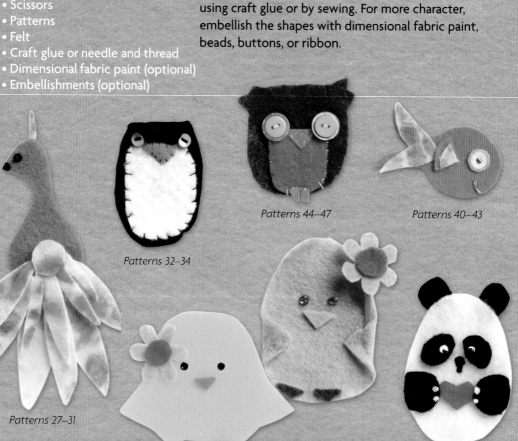

Patterns 44–47

Patterns 40–43

Patterns 32–34

Patterns 27–31

Patterns 48–50

Patterns 35–39

Pets

Darling Dachshund

Create the perfect puppy pal.

You will need:
- 🖐️ Help from an adult
- Scissors
- Wrapping-paper tube
- Felt
- Glue or double-stick tape
- Pencil
- Patterns

1. With help from an adult, cut a wrapping-paper tube so that it is 4 inches long. Wrap a piece of felt around tube and attach with glue or double-stick tape. Cut off any excess felt.

2. With help from an adult, cut off one end of the tube on a diagonal.

3. Trace and cut out Patterns 51 through 54 from felt. Glue small circles for the eyes and nose onto the face. Then glue the face to the diagonal end of the tube.

4. Trace and cut out a circle to cover the end of the tube. Sandwich the tail between this piece and the tube with glue. Finish by gluing on the ears and legs. Add a pretty bow and let dry.

Sweet Tweet

A beautiful birdie made by you.

You will need:
- Pencil
- Patterns
- Felt in multiple colors
- Scissors
- Glue
- Embroidery needle
- Embroidery floss
- 2 buttons
- Stuffing

1. Trace and cut out 2 bird body shapes using Pattern 77. Trace and cut out 4 wings using Pattern 79, 2 in one color and 2 in a second color.

2. Layer one wing of each color on top of the other and glue. Then glue both wings to the bird's body. Repeat on the other side.

3. Glue or sew on buttons for eyes, Pattern 78 triangles for a beak, and 2 thin rectangles for legs.

4. Use the Whip Stitch (instructions on page 6) to sew the two body pieces together. Leave a small opening to insert stuffing. When the bird is stuffed enough, finish sewing it closed.

Funny Bunny

See who's hopping this way.

You will need:
- ✋ Help from an adult
- Scissors
- Wrapping-paper tube
- Felt (multiple colors)
- Glue or double-stick tape
- Pencil
- Patterns
- Dimensional fabric paint

1. With help from an adult, cut a wrapping-paper tube so that it is 5 inches long (or 3 inches for a baby bunny). Wrap a piece of felt around the tube and attach with glue or double-stick tape. Cut off any excess felt.

2. With help from an adult, cut off one end of the tube on a diagonal.

3. Trace and cut out Pattern 57 from felt. Attach this face piece to the tube with craft glue. Trace and cut out Patterns 58 and 59 for the ears. Attach the ears to the head.

4. Trace and cut out Patterns 55, 56, and 60, as well as a small teardrop shape for the nose. Glue on all of the pieces and let dry. Add dimensional fabric paint for eyes.

Bear Buddy

This stuffed cub is a real softie.

You will need:
- Pencil
- Scissors
- Patterns
- Felt in multiple colors
- Glue
- Embroidery needle
- Embroidery floss
- 4 buttons
- Yarn
- Stuffing
- Decorative-edge scissors (optional)

1. Trace and cut out 2 bear bodies, 2 ears, and 2 arms using Patterns 71, 75, 76, and 80. Trace and cut out one each of Patterns 70, 72, 73, and 74.

2. To one body piece, glue on the bear snout, belly, and hearts. Glue or sew on buttons for eyes, a nose, and a belly button.

3. When glue is dry, flip the piece over and glue the ears, arms, and yarn hair to the back of the piece. Let dry.

4. Use the Whip and Running Stitches (instructions on page 6) to sew the two body pieces together. Leave a small opening to insert stuffing. When the bear is stuffed enough, finish sewing it closed.

Mighty Cute Monkey

Check out who's hanging around.

You will need:
- Pencil
- Scissors
- Patterns
- Felt in multiple colors
- Glue
- Sewing needle
- Thread
- Stuffing

1. Trace and cut out 2 each of Patterns 64, 66, and 68 from felt. Trace and cut out 1 each of Patterns 61, 67, and 69. Trace and cut out the flower pieces using Patterns 62 and 63.

2. Glue piece 67 on top of 66, and piece 69 on top of 68. When dry, glue the 2 pieces together to make the face.

3. Trace and cut out Patterns 12 and 13 for the eyes, Pattern 61 for the mouth, and 2 small squares for the nose. Glue on the face pieces. When dry, glue the ears to the back of the head. Let dry.

4. Use the Whip and Running Stitches (instructions on page 6) to sew the two head pieces together. Leave a small opening to insert stuffing. When stuffed enough, finish sewing closed. Glue the flower pieces above one of the monkey's ears.

Food

Perfect Petit Fours

Tiny desserts look sweet enough to eat.

You will need:
- Pencil
- Patterns
- Felt in multiple colors
- Scissors
- 1-inch wood cubes
- Glue or double-stick tape
- Rickrack
- Mini-cupcake wrappers

Trace Pattern 81 onto felt and cut out. Wrap the felt around a 1-inch cube, and attach using glue or double-stick tape. Glue a piece of rickrack around the outside. Trace Patterns 12 and 19 and cut out felt shapes. Glue shapes to the top to look like fruit or flowers. When glue is dry, place petit four in a mini-cupcake wrapper. Repeat to make more petit fours.

Cutout Cookies

No-bake cookies are sure to be a crowd-pleaser.

You will need:
- Pencil
- Scissors
- Patterns
- Felt in multiple colors
- Craft glue
- Embellishments (optional)

Make a big batch of cookies by cutting out various circle and heart patterns from felt. Layer the circle shapes with frosting-colored felt, and top with beads for sprinkles. Cut out a smaller heart shape from the center of the large heart shape of Pattern 82. Glue the cutout heart on top of a full heart and use yarn or other embellishments to make fake filling. Get creative and see what other kinds of cookies you can "bake"!

Super Slices

Have a heaping serving of fake cake or pie!

You will need:
- Patterns
- Tape
- Felt in multiple colors
- Glue stick or double-stick tape
- Pencil
- Scissors
- Pinking shears
- #1 Craft glue
- Embellishments (optional)

1. Punch out Pattern 85 for pie or 86 for cake. (You may want to make a copy of these before making this craft.) Fold along the score lines and tape in place.

2. Wrap the sides with a strip of felt and attach with a glue stick or double-stick tape. Using the base as a guide, mark and cut out top and bottom pieces, and glue or tape them to the folded edges.

3. Using the base as a guide, mark a back piece. Add ¼ inch to the height and cut out. Trim the top edge with pinking shears. Glue or tape this piece to the back of the base.

4. Decorate your cake or pie slice with additional felt shapes or beads. For a fruit filling, glue on embroidery floss in swirly shapes. For whipped cream, see the Sewn Flower instructions on page 13.

Cupcake Cuties

Decorating these desserts is the best part.

You will need:
- Template
- Felt (in multiple colors)
- Double-stick tape
- Scissors
- Pinking shears
- Craft glue
- Pencil
- Large pom-poms
- Wavy-edge scissors (optional)
- Sewing needle (optional)
- Thread (optional)
- Stuffing

1. Punch out Template 84. (You may want to make a copy of this before making this craft.) Attach this piece to felt with double-stick tape.

2. Cut the felt out around the Template piece. Cut with pinking shears across the long edge. With the felt side facing out, wrap the ends around and glue together.

3. When dry, trace the bottom of the cupcake base onto felt. Cut out and craft glue to the bottom. When dry, stuff the inside of the cup with a pom-pom to look like cake.

4. Add a frosting top. For the white-top cupcake, cut out Patterns 8, 9, and 10 with wavy-edge scissors. Cut a slit to the center of each circle. Overlap and craft glue the edges to create a dome shape. Glue all layers together.

5. For the pink cupcake, whipstitch two Pattern 8 circles together. Stuff and sew closed. For the blue cupcake, layer Patterns 8, 9, and 10 with a dot of craft glue in the middle of each. Fluff and glue to a pom-pom.

Sweet Cinnamon Rolls

Serve up a yummy-looking breakfast treat.

You will need:
- Felt (2 colors of brown)
- Scissors
- Ruler
- Double-stick tape or glue
- White dimensional fabric paint

1. From each felt color, cut out a 4-by-10-inch strip. Fold each strip in half lengthwise, and tape or glue in place.

2. Tape or glue one folded piece on top of the other. Run tape or glue along one strip and tightly roll from the end. Trim off edges to be even.

3. Top the cinnamon roll with white dimensional fabric paint to look like icing. Let dry. Repeat to make more cinnamon rolls.

Tasty Toast

Butter up a super slice.

You will need:
- Pencil
- Scissors
- Patterns
- Felt in multiple colors
- Craft glue

Trace and cut out of felt 4 pieces of Pattern 83. Glue the layers together. Cut out a strip of felt that is ¼ inch wider than the thickness of the toast. Apply glue to this strip and attach it to the outside of the toast. Glue on a few layers of yellow square felt to look like butter.

Show us or tell us about
your funky felt creations!

Send them to:

Funky Felt Crafts Editor
American Girl
8400 Fairway Place
Middleton, WI 53562

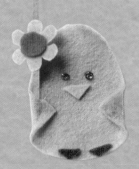

Here are some other American Girl books you might like:

❏ *I read it.*

❏ *I read it.*

❏ *I read it.*

❏ *I read it.*

❏ *I read it.*

Patterns